Lessons We've Learned

T.F. and Thetus Tenney

Copyright © 2019 T.F. and Thetus Tenney

All rights reserved.

ISBN: 9781689430548

CONTENTS

Prologue   v

Some Things About Seasons   1
and Other Things I Have Learned Along the Way

Some Things I've Learned   35

PROLOGUE

As we all live through our individual lives there are lessons to be learned along the way. The more you learn, the easier some aspects of life become. I am approaching the halfway mark of my eighth decade; I hope my sharing of "Some Things I Have Learned Along the Way" will help readers gain insights to help them on their own journeys where ever they may presently be along the way.

I received the Holy Ghost on January 30, 1942. I like to tell this story because it is a word of encouragement to everyone involved in teaching children. When I was 10 years old there was a new convert in our church who came to my parents, asking if she could start a class for children. She started it on Sunday afternoons. She had no teaching experience, and did not have access to any of the helps we now have for teaching. Yet, on a rainy Sunday afternoon when there were only a few children there, she stood in front of us and talked about presenting our bodies, holy, acceptable unto the Lord. It was in that setting the Lord spoke to my heart and I felt a call into ministry. Though I did not know at that time what it all meant, or where answering that call would take me, it was real. Don't ever forget that God deals with children. There is more to children being in church than just providing entertainment for them. Their hearts are open and often they are more accepting than adults. Don't neglect to notice that God deals with them.

I have been a student of the word for over 70 years. I was 12 years old when I decided it was time for me to get serious about reading and studying the Bible. I have been teaching the Bible and lessons from it for over 68 years. When I was 15 years old, I started a backyard Bible club and I ended up with 30, 40 and 50 children, sitting out on the grass. I am still in touch with some of those children – now all grown up.

My age indicates this is probably my last season of life. I am doing my best to assure when I leave this world, that I have done my best and accomplished everything assigned to me to do for the Kingdom.

-Thetus Tenney

SOME THINGS ABOUT SEASONS
and Other Things I've Learned Along the Way

THETUS TENNEY

SOME THINGS ABOUT SEASONS
and Other Things I Have Learned Along the Way

Seasons are God's idea. All creation is governed by seasons. There is a rhythm in seasons and that rhythm makes progressions smoother. Life is a succession of seasons. This one simple statement has been one of the strongest underpinnings of my life. It is, perhaps, the most important thing I have learned along the way. Just like winter, spring, summer, and fall the seasons of life come and go, in their own time and in their own way. If you do not get a simple understanding of the principle of seasons, you will find yourself living in frustration about the facts and factors of the seasons of your life.

You cannot do all things in all seasons. All seasons have certain facets in everyone's life while also possessing other qualities that are as unique to the individual as their fingerprints. For some things, their season will pass never to come again. For others, you will see them ahead but have to wait for that "due season" to come in order to truly grasp their value. Some things may even be present in all seasons. What happens in one season affects the next one.

Through the years, I have lived the seasons of my own life – and observed them in the lives of others. Sometimes I've seen the season change very well-defined. In other times, I've seen the seasons overlap. Sometimes there is an early spring or an Indian summer. Sometimes in the midst of winter, there can be a glimpse of spring to come but not yet – it comes just bringing hope that it won't be dark and cold forever. The sun will shine and the flowers will bloom again.

For the sake of this writing, I am sharing what I have seen as the seasons correlate with the decades of life.

THE 20s

In your twenties, you are deciding who you are and He is molding what you will become. You are discovering your gifts - finding out what you can do and, just as important, what you don't need to do. It is in your twenties you are drawn toward things that feed your passion. It is in this season your personality finds unique expression.

Giftings are very important; God placed them in each of us for a reason. No one is born giftless. In your twenties you are observing others – some in the same season you are – and some in the seasons yet to come. You are feeling things you may not have felt before. Your future is calling you out of immaturity and preparing you for your destiny. The foundation of what you will be – who you will become in the Kingdom of God – is being developed in the days of this season of your twenties.

Giftings are not hidden. Whatever it is you enjoy doing, whatever you have a "leaning" toward – *that* is your God-given gifting. Your gifts are what God gives you; developing those gifts and using them for the Kingdom are what you give back to Him. I have to admit I have observed people in their forties and even fifties who seem to still be trying to identify their gifts – when those gifts have been obvious but unrecognized since their twenties or even earlier. Your gifts are not all spiritual, and none of them are buried unless you bury them yourself.

Whatever it is that you enjoy doing, whatever you have a "leaning" toward *that* is your God-given gifting.

THE 30s

In your thirties, you have discovered your gifts and set about developing your potential. The thirties are the season in which you do the work of polishing the gifts you have been given. The Old Testament instructions for the building of the Tabernacle makes reference repeatedly to skilled craftsmen. It is in your thirties that you begin to hone your skills in whatever field of labor He has called you.

Remember, God sees us as Kingdom people. We are not here just living life for life's sake. We are building the Kingdom in this life, that we may rule and reign with Him in the life to come.

It was in my thirties I became certain that teaching was one of my primary giftings. It was what I wanted to do the rest of my life. It was during these years I loved my Sunday School classes and Bible study groups. Teaching settings of any kind brought me great joy and fulfillment. I loved the study and preparation; I loved the act of teaching; I loved the interaction with students. I began to discover my gifting even as a teenager teaching Children's Church and Sunday School – and by my thirties I was learning to walk in that calling.

That was where I fit. Even today, it is still my gifting. I know, because I am comfortable with it and I love doing it.

THE 40s

It is in your forties when you determine the direction for the rest of your life. You are on the edge of the most important and productive years you will ever have. The forties are strenuous and stressful. The forties are the stepping stone to what your whole legacy will become. It is the open door to "the rest of your life." It is essential you realize you are on the edge of your most productive years in your 40s.

My husband believed and often said, "The most productive years of ministry are between 45 and 65." That is when you need to make life really count. Time is precious and the years move swiftly.

THE 50s

The fifties are the season of distilling. The essence of who you are has been established and is lived out in the day to day. The fifties are the season of "moving on up." These are busy years and the "backbone" of your life.

In the season of your fifties you are finally and finely defining your life.

THE 60s

The sixties will make the big statement of your life. You only have one life and if it is not spent for kingdom purposes, you have virtually wasted it, and will pass into the closing seasons burdened with regret. To quote my husband again, it is in these "middle seasons" that you must remind yourself of the old adage: "If you can touch it; it will not last." Bank accounts, cars, careers, houses, clothes, fun, all of those things we do in life, none of it will last into eternity. We must not spend our lives on temporal things but focus instead on the things of eternal value. Be careful how you use your life.

You still have the vim and vigor, you still have the get-up-and-go. You have learned a lot, and the sixties are very important for production in the Kingdom. Don't waste these years by saying, "I am getting older, I've done my part." Or, "I am 65, I am ready to take it easy…I am ready to rest and let someone else do the work." That is not what God intends for you in this season. You have learned a lot, matured and developed your gifts. The sixties are the best years of your life for making a big difference for the Kingdom.

God wants you to recognize this and utilize these years to make a lasting impact.

THE 70s

It is in your seventies when you display the totality of who you are. You are definitely headed home, on the downward slope of the mountain of your life whether you want to admit it or not. Your energy level is declining but not depleted. Profiting from past seasons, these can be the best years of your life. Your children are grown and you're enjoying grandchildren and the "greats" may even be present in this decade. In my personal experience, for both me and my husband, we enjoyed this season as one of our best. Change directions, reach beyond what you've been doing to do something else, but don't retire and stay home. Keep active. Keep moving. Keep living. Enjoy the ride!

THE 80s

Then you hit the eighties, the season I find myself in now . . . at least for a few more years. In the eighties, it is time to abdicate your positions and move to the bleachers. You are not leaving the game; you are just changing positions. Just because you're not on the playing field doesn't mean you are not integral to the game. Your role now is to clap and cheer for the generations coming behind you.

Let your continued enthusiasm infuse expectancy into younger friends. Commit yourself to encourage and not criticize. Share positive thoughts and ideas – give them words of strength and encouragement. Share your wisdom and knowledge and experience with them. God is not finished with you yet.

THE 90s

There is one more season we are all headed for, should God be willing. That is, the years of our nineties. This is the season I've labeled "Adoration." Steps are slower. There may be health issues. Memories may be fading. However, remember Anna in the story of the early days of the life of Jesus Christ? She was in her ninth decade. She spent her time in the temple, continually praising God. When we reach our nineties, we are still not done. While physical strength is diminished and stamina is limited, praise can flow forth from you with great ease. It is not a place from which you judge or criticize the younger ones around you. Adore Him. Give yourself to His praise. You will then find no time left for muttering about "this younger generation."

God is the God of the new as well as the old. When you criticize a new thing or a young person who is "not doing it like you did," you may be criticizing something or somebody God has been waiting on for a long time. Be careful you don't get hardening of the attitudes while you are getting hardening of the arteries. Change is inevitable. Accept it.

As stated earlier, what you are is God's gift to you. What you become with those gifts is your gift to Him. There are many very gifted people who have never learned to interpret those gifts into kingdom enterprise. Whatever gifts you have, everything from cooking to working on cars, can be used for Kingdom enterprise. If you are using those gifts for other purposes and not using them for the Kingdom, you are misusing God's gifts.

Find a way to interpret your giftings into Kingdom enterprise. If you are a good mechanic, those gifts can be used for helping the widows, keeping the church buses running. Do you enjoy serving people? The gift of hospitality is recognized four times in the New Testament. Any gifts, big or small, can be interpreted into the work of the Kingdom.

Attention and understanding of your present season will always make the next season better.

Seasons are inevitable. Neglect of care in one season can make the next season more difficult. Jesus spoke of "fruit" – "more fruit" – and "much fruit." We are part of an ever increasing Kingdom.

Whatever your season, give attention to it. Don't compare your season with someone else. Seasons are for development and are designed to develop us into what God has planned for us individually. It is not wise to compare ourselves among ourselves (II Corinthians 10:12). Be the best 'you' God intended you to be.

Don't wish for the next season – or a new season - while you are in the one that precedes it. Every season has a specific purpose. In younger years, with a young family, don't try to do everything you will be able to do in later years. Don't compromise your present season by trying to harvest from a future season

Seasons are really a very simple concept, giving us a kind of skeleton-look at our lives. This concept of seasons came to me when I was very young and it has meant much to me.

Life will take you through all the seasons. You will thrive in some and struggle in others. There will be cold, dark winters but there will also be the hope-filled days of spring. You will come to readily recognize the seasons in your own life. You will also begin seeing the seasons lived out in the lives of your children and others.

In addition to the bedrock lessons of "the seasons", there are some other practical lessons I have learned along the way about myself, about others, about serving God and His working in my life.

> *Know who you are; know who you aren't.*

When I was young, if you were going to marry a preacher, there were two requirements: You had to sing and you had to play an accordion. My mother preached a little revival and came home with an extra $100 and bought me a used accordion. God knows I tried! It wasn't my calling and it certainly wasn't my gifting. That relic of my teen years is in the Historical Museum on the Louisiana District campground in Tioga! Music was something I could do, but it was a struggle. It was not my gifting. It is not only important that you know who you are but be sure you know who you aren't.

Pastors and church leaders need to be especially aware of the giftings of the people they are working with – who they are and who they aren't. As church structure and staff for ministries are being developed, it is vitally important that the people

Lessons We've Learned

match the task at hand. For instance, a person who feels a special affinity for teenagers and young adults, probably should not be assigned to work in the nursery. The person who is gifted musically and wants more than anything to "play skillfully before the Lord" will be frustrated and frustrate those around him or her if they are assigned to the janitorial crew. However, the lady who loves the smell of Mr. Clean and who gets an incredible sense of satisfaction when a sink and countertop sparkle – and is terrified of public speaking – will thrive on the cleaning staff and resign from teaching the 3-year-olds.

It is important for you to know who you are. God has a place for you. Don't try to be somebody you are not supposed to be. Become the best you that you can be. Don't let anyone else write your Kingdom job description. However, there may be times you will need to serve in positions uncomfortable for you. Do your best as you learns lessons of submission and humility.

> *Your turn will come, whatever it is.*

Look at the story of Moses. I marvel how Moses endured life. He had the best of everything and then he had nothing. Yet, when he saw the burning bush, he said, "Now, will I turn..." Your turn will come. If you are following the will of God, if you are seeking after the will of God, I promise you, your turn will come. It may not come in the same age that your friend's did. It may not come at the time you think it should. I can just promise if you are following God, He will not fail to bring you into what He has intended for you. All you have to do is be sensitive to His calling and His direction "in all thy ways." You are not without purpose. You were made for a purpose – designed by God to fulfill a destiny that serves Him and completes you.

Paul compares the Christian life to a walk. Keep moving – simply putting one foot in front of the other one. You have a pre-determined destiny – and He knows the end from the beginning. Within each of us lies a sense of destiny. Sometimes we recognize it readily; sometimes we have to seek for it. Ask a 6-year-old what they want to be. They are dreaming and their answers reflect that: I want to be a pilot; I want to be a doctor. How old are you in the Lord? Are you still dreaming? Are you still reaching? God has a plan and a destiny for you. Don't stop short of His plans. God's Kingdom is an everlasting Kingdom.

> *Balance is valuable.*

Another vitally important thing I've learned along the way is *the value of balance.* Balance in life is one of the most important things one can learn and practice. People can get out of balance really quickly – but can also get back in balance just as fast. Remember that balance is never done once and for all. You are constantly shifting a little here and moving a little there to achieve balance.

Remember the see-saw or teeter-totter at the playground when you were a kid? All the time you are on the seesaw, it's up and down. Sometimes you played on it with someone else participating in the up and down of it all. Sometimes you "walked the plank" and tried to stand just right in the middle for the board to be straight and balanced. It was always a struggle.

Staying balanced in life is very important! Thessalonians 5:23 says He will sanctify us wholly — spirit and soul and body; all of you is sanctified by the "very God of peace." All of "us" – of life – is sacred. Understanding this will bring peace. The most peaceful people you will find are men and women who have learned the value of balance in their lives. Balance is not set; it is in a constant state of being maintained. Sometimes one thing requires more attention than another. The next week, that very thing "on the back burner" the week before will be what requires your attention today. That is why it is important to pay attention to the seasons of your life. Understanding the seasons will help you understand how to strike your balance for that time in your life and in the season in which you are living.

When I was a young woman, my husband was traveling all over the world with his work. We lived in a house out at the edge of the woods. I had one neighbor. I cannot tell you how many times I felt so alone and left out. Tom was flying off to some faraway place, preaching the Gospel, winning the lost. I was home changing diapers, washing clothes, mothering and homemaking. God helped me with that. I am so grateful God helped me know what to do in that season besides just the obvious.

Although I did not realize it at the time, it was during those years I actually prepared the foundation for everything I have done since then. For seven years I was at home alone much of the time with my young children. My heart was yearning to be involved in the Kingdom of God. All the gifts I have ever had were within me. I could feel them stirring. I felt urged to do something, but didn't know exactly what I could do. The Lord helped me, and I soon decided to spend my time studying.

You remember I said you need to know who you are and who you aren't? Well, I quickly learned that I am not a night person. If I tried to stay up late to study, I would hear noises outside that frightened me. So, I developed a better daily routine. I would straighten the house before settling down for the night, then make sure I got to bed early. Then, two or three hours before time to wake the children, I would get up and spend that time studying, reading, and praying.

I actually read study books that were a great deal beyond my understanding. I would read for hours – praying and reading, reading and praying. I learned so much about the Word of God then that the next season, I had a foundation to build on. Every season offers something upon which you can build your future. Take advantage of it and know balance in life is important. How we use the seasons of our lives is important. Don't neglect the things that are in your season.

> *The older people need to understand the seasons of the younger people.*

Another thing that is important is *for the older people to understand the seasons of the younger people.* Don't expect a young mother, whether she be a pastor's wife or a saint in the church, to be at every little meeting you have if she has three or four little kids. It is the season for her to give herself to those children. It is a seasonal life and balance is very important. Sanctify your whole spirit and soul and body - and you will know the God of peace. Peace comes with those things. Secular and sacred are always homogenized. You interpret all of life by kingdom standards. The scriptures say, "You serve the Lord - and that we do all in the name of the Lord Jesus."

> *Understand this, the secular and the sacred are homogenized.*

God is in all of life, *all* of life. The only life you have is the breath He put inside of you. He is in every bit of life, regardless of what it is, whether taking care of kids, or standing in a pulpit, it is all God-related. The more you can see life like that, the more it makes sense and the easier it is to find and do what you are God-created to do.

> *Your job description depends on where you are.*

Descriptions can vary from season to season. I have heard Martha demeaned because she was in the kitchen. In truth, Jesus reproved her attitude not her work. There would have been no supper that night if Martha had not been in the kitchen. Whatever you are doing, if your attitude is as serving the Lord, then He puts that down as you doing what He wants you to do. So there are kitchens and altars.

You can make your kitchen an altar; serve there as unto the Lord.

Thomas à Kempis, an old priest in Europe, spent his time in the monastery in the kitchen. His primary task was washing the dishes. He was also a prolific copier and writer. He wrote a little book called, "The Imitation of Christ" in 1441. Today it is still considered one of the most read books of Christianity worldwide, second only to the Bible itself. He had a servant's heart and was willing to wash the dishes of his brethren while also devoting the rest of his time to the creative work of writing what he was living. He wrote, "Be thankful for the least gift, so shalt thou be meant to receive greater." He had a keen understanding of seasons, gifts, and balance.

I'd like to take the time here to tell a personal story. It was a time when God spoke clearly to me and left a mark of understanding of this concept. In the 1980s, while my husband served as the District Superintendent over the United Pentecostal Churches and ministers of the state of Louisiana, I began to host conferences for women on the District Campground. At the time, it was one of the largest women's conferences that had been held to date in the US. It was the first night of the Conference. We were past capacity in the building. The aisles were filled and there seemed no way through the crowd.

At the close of the service, my husband came to rescue me and take me home. We walked from the platform up the choir loft stairs. We crossed through a meeting room, and were able to exit the building into a car waiting to drive us home.

When I got there, my daughter and my daughter-in-law who were both helping me with the conference, and were both mothers of toddlers, were already there. Their two little girls were tired and fussy. Knowing it was bath time, I took one of the wee ones to my room and put her in my bathtub. I bathed her, dried her off, and put her in her little nightgown. I gathered her up in my arms and walked back into the den. The other little girl came wandering in from having been through the same routine with her mother in the upstairs bath. I picked up the second granddaughter, and sank into my rocking chair. Holding both girls in my lap I began to rock and sing a lullaby.

I can tell you even today, if the Lord has ever spoken to me, He spoke to me that night. "What you are doing now is as much in my will as when you stood tonight before those thousands of women." It was a benchmark in my life; I have never forgotten. The Lord saw me as a grandmother taking care of the babies as fulfilling His will, just as much as if I were leading that women's conference. "As unto the least of these..." (Matthew 25:40).

> *If all of life is seen as God-ordained it will make a difference in how you feel about everything you do, from the mundane to the magnificent.*

Everything we do, if it is interpreted in the Kingdom realm, is important. God created Adam and Eve. He placed them in the Garden of Eden and instructed them to care for it. That was their God-gifting and God-command. If you will interpret all of life into Kingdom enterprise it will give meaning to all of life.

> *Never let life go stale.*

Life is a beautiful gift from God. It is the preparatory time for eternal life and has much meaning. We should cherish life and care for it in all aspects as a precious gift from God. God ordained life and marriage; he didn't ordain for you to get tired of it either. He meant for you to work at it. Don't let your marriage grow stale; don't let your work grow stale. Don't let your Kingdom life grow stale.

We must never let our relationship with God grow stale

It is of primary importance *we never let our relationship with God grow stale.* Keep it fresh. God so wanted a relationship with us that He entered into earthly life so we could relate to Him. We must value our relationship with Him; we must learn to converse with Him. No relationship can ever survive without conversation. Prayer is the conversation between God and us. Purposeful, relational, meaningful prayer is essential to a growing relationship with God.

Many years ago I came to know that prayer is not a "Give me..." and "I want..." and "Will you help me..." thing. Prayer is time to go to the Lord with the primary motive being fellowship with Him. Express sincere thanks to Him for all He has done for you. Talk about how wonderful He is. Ask for His help and His wisdom. He knows we have needs and will receive our requests but the simple fellowship of His Spirit with our spirit is beyond price. Prayer is a conversation, not a monologue. Don't be so rude to Him that you never hush and allow Him speak. In quietness and meditation your relationship with God is enhanced. Prayer should never grow stale.

When Paul was knocked down on the road to Damascus, he asked, "Who art thou, Lord?" Jesus answered him, saying, "I am Jesus..." Jesus introduced Himself to Paul on a first-name basis. First name friends have a close relationship. It is what Jesus wants.

He wants a relationship with you – a living, thriving, growing relationship that will last your entire lifetime and into eternity.

We are the bride of Christ. The Old Testament called Israel the wife of Jehovah. Do you know the difference between a bride and a wife? They do a lot of the same things, fit the same definitions. However, there is a difference – it is a difference in attitude. The bride is thrilled and excited and happy to do things, even the little things that bring her into her husband's favor. The wife, though, is often taken so much with the duty and the drudgery of everyday life, she has lost the delight of "I'm my beloved's and he is mine." Don't lose the wonder of the Wonderful One! He is your bridegroom; you are His bride. Your relationship with Him – and His with you – should be loving, nurturing, exciting.

Talk to the Lord like you would talk to a friend. Have you ever examined your personal prayer words – to discover you are repeating words you don't really mean? Or, are you saying words repetitiously with little meaning? Even the child's mealtime prayer invites some thoughtful clarification: "God is great. . ." How is He great? What has He done for you that demonstrates His greatness? "God is good . . ." Why do you say that He is good? How has He demonstrated in your life that He is a good God? "Let us thank Him for our food..." Thank Him for vegetables and meat and potatoes? We need to think about what we say to Him and when we say it. Meaningful conversations build meaningful relationships. Never, at any season of life, should our relationship with God grow stale or monotonous.

Tomorrow depends on today.

I have learned that *tomorrow depends on today.* Four times in the Scriptures it says, "To day if you will hear His voice..." Not many things are repeated four times in the scriptures, but "To day if you will hear His voice..." is repeated four times. Life has no practice moments. What is said and done today has a lasting effect on tomorrow . . . and the day after . . . and the day after. We must pay attention to what we are doing – where we are going – what we are saying. We must get it right today, in order for it to be right tomorrow.

You will repeat the lessons you don't learn.

Another important truth I have learned is this: *You will repeat the lessons you don't learn.* I have been around a few mountains many times before I learned the intended lesson. Remember, the children of Israel went around the same mountain for 40 years in the wilderness and kept repeating the same mistakes. When you don't learn a lesson, you have to repeat it. Tests have purpose. Tests are not meant to fail us; rather, they are to advance us. If the same kind of problem keeps happening there may be a lesson you aren't learning.

It is important to learn how to handle criticism.

Criticism will come. When somebody says something bad about you or about your work, don't be quick to judge them. Try to understand what they saw that triggered their statements. Look below the surface and find why what was said was said. The scriptures teach us, in Proverbs 21:2, that men do what is right in their own eyes. They may or may not be right; they think they are right. My husband made sure I learned a difficult lesson along those lines. He said to me, "Quit judging what they said and see why they said it." If you will do this, it will give you understanding.

> *Everyone will not love you;*
> *however, you can love everyone.*

This may be an amazing revelation for you, but here it is: *Everyone will not love you; however, you can love everyone.* It is possible to love those you may not like. There will be some people you just cannot develop a relationship with and others you work to keep a relationship with. My husband used to say, "I am allergic to some people." Some people just don't fit with you, your life and your season. However, don't judge them harshly. The reality is you are not fitting into their life either. Be nice to those you are "allergic" to, guard your comments and wish them well. Don't waste your time and energy on a relationship God has not brought to you.

> *Friends are a worthy investment.*

I have learned *friends are a worthy investment.* Everyone needs someone who knows them for who they really are – without titles or positions. Real friends help ground you. Real friends help heal hurts. Friends can help restore confidence. Real friendship requires the investment of time; it is a worthy investment.

Remember the example lived out by Jesus. He had the multitudes – the twelve – the three within the twelve – and then just John remaining at the foot of the cross. He had degrees of relationship. So will we. One writer observed, "In your entire life, you can probably count your true friends on one hand. Maybe even on one finger. Those are the friends you need to cherish, and I wouldn't trade one of them for a hundred of the other kind..." (Sarah Ockler on goodreads.com).

> *Life is a journey with a predetermined destiny.*

Before you were even born, God determined your destiny. The scripture speaks of being "fearfully and wonderfully made" (Psalm 139:14). God knew us before we ever saw our first day. He predetermined the course of our life on earth and into the Kingdom. I believe God predetermined our destiny. It then becomes our responsibility to keep walking, one step at a time, following the course He planned to reach the destiny He intended.

It doesn't take a whole lot of sense to walk. You just have to know how to put one foot in front of the other and keep doing it. That is the process of walking. If we follow the steps ordered of the Lord, those steps will lead us to the place He has predetermined for us.

Change is inevitable.

God never changes in His attributes and character – but He is also a God of change. Moses had a stick. He did everything with his stick, one man with one stick. Joshua had a committee. He had the group of priests step into the water. Moses lifted that stick and the Red Sea parted. Joshua and his committee put their feet into the edge of the water and the Jordan River parted. This was a significant change in "the way we do things." According to Isaiah 43:19, the never-changing God can and will do a new thing: "Behold, I will do a new thing; now it shall spring forth; shall ye not know it? I will even make a way in the wilderness, and rivers in the desert."

Solitude is needful.

The scriptures teach us there is strength in quietness. Isaiah 30:15 reminds us, "For thus saith the Lord GOD, the Holy One of Israel; In returning and rest shall ye be saved; in quietness and in confidence shall be your strength…"

Paul advises us to learn to be quiet (I Thessalonians 4:11). Jesus only had five-and-a-half years of active ministry, but he took time to withdraw from the busyness of life and ministry to a solitary place and prayed.

> *Don't waste a crisis.*

Every crisis can serve a purpose. None of us enjoys a crisis or troublesome times, but finding what can be learned from the situation can make a hard time profitable.

> *I have learned life is enriched by taking pleasure in small things.*

Even Jesus talked about the flowers of the field. God made a big world. Love it, notice it. Have you ever done anything you thought was especially good and nobody noticed? I wonder sometimes if God looks down and sees us so busy we haven't even noticed all He is doing and has done for us. Enjoy creation. Enjoy what God has done. Sunrises and sunsets – every day a new masterpiece is painted for us. Don't let too many of them pass without noticing and thanking Him!

> *Get your direction from the altar.*

There is a scripture that speaks of north of the altar. Get all of your direction from the altar. There is nowhere that prayer can be eliminated.

Lessons We've Learned

We all need two altars in our lives. When the children of Israel were going in to occupy their promised land, they built two altars. They were made from heavy stones carried on the shoulders of the priests. Many altars are built from the hard and heavy things of life. They built one altar in the river bed while the river was parted. The other was built on the other side of Jordan.

The altar in the riverbed was soon buried beneath the flow of the waters, never to be seen again. Some things need to be buried at an altar never to be remembered again. The other altar was built on the edge of their tomorrow. It sanctified the future and was a reminder of God's help in the past.

Build an altar to forget with. Then build another altar on the edge of your tomorrow. This is the altar you can show your children and say, "I remember when God..." Let the past be the past except for praise.

> *There is no end to learning and becoming.*

The scripture speaks of "the increase of His government" in Isaiah 9:7. I know we usually think that refers to a spiritual realm of things. Remember, though, He is the governor of your life. The longer you live for Him, the more governed by Him your life should be. There is no end to His government in the world and in us. It should be ever increasing in every aspect of our lives.

Learn to live in joy.

This is not always easy for me. However, the value of living in joy is an important lesson I have learned along the way. Joy is a sure sign of faith. Intercessors sometimes have a tendency toward depression. They carry heavy burdens and the weight of it sometimes overpowers them. Yet, it is possible, even if you are an intercessor, to end your prayer time with a time of rejoicing about the good things God has done and will do for you. This will bring joy to your heart – and that joy is a sign of your faith. You cannot really believe God is going to do something for you without feeling the joy of the Lord. "The joy of the Lord is my strength..." (Nehemiah 8:10). Joy brings strength for the journey.

I've shared here "Some Things I Have Learned Along the Way." There have been other lessons – hard lessons learned even within this list of things – yet, through them all He has proved Himself to be a loving Savior, full of grace and truth and peace. I believe even now, as I am in the middle of my 80s, that God still has big plans for me to accomplish before I die. I am grateful to be saved from hell. However, that is not what motivates me. What motivates me is that He has saved me unto life everlasting where I will rule and reign with Him forever.

I close this writing with a prayer for every reader:

God, I pray You will keep us. We simply give you permission to take over our lives, hearts, and minds. Let us train our minds, our hearts, our spirits to understand the ways of the Kingdom. Help us to understand it is your Kingdom that we are destined to inherit. We must know the laws of that Kingdom; we must set ourselves to learn them. I pray for every person who has picked up this little book. May the writings found herein – simple though the words may be – give them strength and direction. May we all continue faithfully, growing, changing, leading, helping until someday we stand together around your throne. On that day, we will all know the journey was worth it all. Thank you for your love for us. Thank you for your care for us. Thank you for your faithfulness toward us. In Jesus Name, Amen

SOME THINGS I'VE LEARNED

T. F. TENNEY

SOME THINGS I'VE LEARNED

Editor's Note: God first gave *Some Things I've Learned* to the heart and mind of T. F. Tenney sometime in the fall of 1997. His notes reflect that he preached it first at a Young Minister's Retreat in Salem, Illinois in January 1998 and last in Memphis, Tennessee at a gathering of the Assemblies of the Lord Jesus Christ in March 2011. Between those times he shared the message in churches and retreats across the United States. In between and after those times, he also shared the concepts and principles of these lessons in public discussions and private counseling sessions.

His wife, Thetus Tenney, wanted to include this message in this booklet with her list of *Lessons Learned Along the Way*. Her prayer is that you will benefit from this "shared wisdom" of a man who closed his notes by saying, "My prayer is that I will continue to learn and some day hear Him say, "Well done…" That day came on June 1, 2018. His words live on, the lessons shared are still invaluable insights into a life well-lived.

-Pamela D. Nolde

◆──────────────◆

One of the most important gems I uncovered in my life was simply this: I've learned that I still have a lot to learn. Though I don't know the source of the quote, I do know it is a profound truth of life: "Learning is not a temporary art but the task of a lifetime." In the process of time, I've learned that you can be young at any age if you plan for the future.

From the vantage point of my seventh decade I want to share with you just some of the skeletons of what I've learned. I understand - and so should you - that my path may not be yours. My comprehension is not infallible. This is the view from my pathway . . . so walk with me for a few minutes. Perhaps my perspective will make your perspective clearer. Perhaps something I've learned – and share with you - will make your life lessons a little easier because you have entered into them with some basic understandings and insights from someone else's journey.

> *Success in the spiritual enterprise is based on commitment*

Commitment can be difficult to define. Webster attempted it with "an agreement or pledge to do something in the future" and "something pledged" and "the state or an instance of being obligated or emotionally impelled." (Merriam-Webster.com). Years ago I heard of a somewhat simple explanation of the difference between investment and commitment. One can invest time and money into something to which they are not truly committed. However, commitment is a once and for all kind of thing. Take a look at a typical American breakfast plate - toast and coffee, eggs and bacon. The chicken made an investment in your breakfast. The pig, however, was committed to it.

True spiritual enterprise requires true commitment to a Kingdom not your own, but His. Jesus Christ said to His disciples in Matthew 16:24: "Then said Jesus unto his disciples, If any man will come after me, let him deny himself, and take up his cross, and follow me." This talk of crosses and denying oneself was not popular among the Jews of His day. It is not so popular among us today. Yet, these are the components of true commitment and the only course of action that will ultimately lead to spiritual success.

Paul wrote to the church at Ephesus a definition of a committed Christian: "That we henceforth be no more children, tossed to and fro, and carried about with every wind of doctrine, by the sleight of men, and cunning craftiness, whereby they lie in wait to deceive; But speaking the truth in love, may grow up into him in all things, which is the head, even Christ: From whom the whole body fitly joined together and compacted by that which every joint supplieth, according to the effectual working in the measure of every part, maketh increase of the body unto the edifying of itself in love" (Ephesians 4:14-16, KJV).

Eugene Peterson, in *The Message*, gave a modern perspective to that passage with these words: "God wants us to grow up, to know the whole truth and tell it in love like Christ in everything. We take our lead from Christ, who is the source of everything we do. He keeps us in step with each other. His very breath and blood flow through us, nourishing us so that we will grow up healthy in God, robust in love."

Emotions can be fickle. Commitment is what keeps you in it for the long haul. Faith is what fuels your commitment.

For the sake of reference, the word "feeling" is recorded twice in the King James text, neither one referring to the "feelings" that sometimes dictate our behavior.

> *Who being past feeling have given themselves over unto lasciviousness, to work all uncleanness with greediness*(Ephesians 4:19).

> *For we have not an high priest which cannot be touched with the feeling of our infirmities; but was in all points tempted like as we are, yet without sin* (Hebrews 4:15).

There is nothing in scripture mentioned about our "feelings" or emotions as a driving force in our thoughts and lives. The word "faith", however, is used 336 times. Faith operates on commitment; feelings operate on emotions. A strong and deep underlying commitment to Jesus Christ will result in a deep commitment to excellence in whatever you do for His kingdom.

A Biblical perspective of commitment is found in the words of Jesus in Luke 14:26: "If any man come to me, and hate not his father, and mother, and wife, and children, and brethren, and sisters, yea, and his own life also, he cannot be my disciple…" Then, in Mark 10:29-30, we read:

> …*Verily I say unto you, There is no man that hath left house, or brethren, or sisters, or father, or mother, or wife, or children, or lands, for my sake, and the gospel's, but he shall receive an hundredfold now in this time, houses, and brethren, and sisters, and mothers, and children, and lands, with persecutions; and in the world to come eternal life.*

Commitment is the exchange of the things of this life for the things of the life to come.

During WWII, Japanese pilots would climb into the cockpit of fighter planes loaded with explosives. Their assignment was to intentionally crash their planes into designated targets. They climbed the ladder and boarded their plane knowing theirs was a suicide missions. It is said that their last cry as they directed the plane to its target was "banzai!" – a shortened version of a word that meant, "Long live the Emperor." That, my friends, is commitment. Misplaced though it is, the willingness to literally give their lives to what they believed was a just cause – to forsake father and mother, sister and brother – that demonstrates for all of us the high cost of commitment.

Lack of commitment seems to be a plague of this day and time, more than any generation before. Not too long ago, men went to work for a company and stayed until they retired. Today, it is not unusual for a person to change jobs seven times or more in a lifetime. I remember product loyalty – when a farmer who owned a Ford truck, traded it in for a new Ford truck, and traded it in for a new Ford truck – and never even shopped the Chevrolet lot. I remember a day when divorce was virtually unheard of, especially in the church. Today, it is almost commonplace. This lack of commitment to anything – a job, a product, another human being can carry itself over into the spiritual life of the individual. However, God wants you to be committed to Him, first and foremost. He wants you to be committed to your wife and family. He wants you to be committed to your church. He wants you to be a committed Christian.

There's a four-letter word that is connected to commitment. It is the answer to many of the dilemmas you will face in life. "Fight or flight" is a basic human response to any threatening situation. When it comes to ministry and marriages, often the answer to that dilemma is simply to STAY. Situations in life will arise that make you want to run. The idea of "cutting your losses" and starting all over again has a definite appeal. Commitment, though, true and deep commitment to the calling of God in your life, may actually dictate that you stay.

Vince Lombardi once observed, "The quality of a person's life is in direct proportion to their commitment to excellence, regardless of their chosen field of endeavor." Be a person committed to excellence in your spiritual life – excellence in prayer and fasting, excellence in your study of the Word, excellence in all aspects of your ministry – and in all aspects of your life both private and public. Your success will be directly proportionate to your commitment. One of the most difficult things to commit to is commitment.

> *Experience is what you get when you don't get what you wanted.*

Admittedly, this may not always be true. However, I have come down certain avenues in life, hit a dead end street, looked back and could honestly say, "Well, at least I had the experience." Thomas Edison attempted over 1,000 different experiments before he discovered incandescent light. He said, "Thank God, now I know a thousand things that won't work." All he had was experience. He had not learned the most important lessons by the things that went right, he learned more and more about incandescent light each time things went wrong.

To further example this, there is a story told about Thomas Edison that reflects his remarkable resilience despite not always getting what he wanted. On December 10, 1914 in West Orange, New Jersey there was a massive explosion. Ten buildings in legendary inventor Thomas Edison's plant, which made up more than half of the site, were engulfed in flames. Between six and eight fire departments rushed to the scene, but the chemical-fueled inferno was too powerful to put out quickly. Mr. Edison's son, Charles, who was 24 at the time got to the scene and found his father calmly watching the blaze and firemen at work. His father looked at him and said, "Go get your mother and all her friends. They'll never see a fire like this again." Charles was a little taken aback at the instruction and wanted to somehow comfort his father. However, Mr. Edison said, "It's all right. We've just got rid of a lot of rubbish."

Henry David Thoreau observed, ""If we will be quiet and ready enough, we shall find compensation in every disappointment." Disappointment will come in life. Don't let it destroy you. Grab the experience – learn from it – and sail on!

> *You need to know where you want to go.*

The Cheshire Cat and Alice in Wonderland had a conversation when she came to the fork in the road. She asked, "Which one should I take?" The Cat then asked her, "Where do you want to go?" She said, "I don't know." He said, "Then it doesn't make any difference." Every man and every woman need goals. A bicycle or a sports car are as useless to a man as a rocket ship if he does not know where he wants to go.

When the boat captain doesn't know what port he's headed to, no wind is the right wind. There is a significant difference between a river and a swamp. A river is going one place; it flows one direction. A swamp, on the other hand, wants to go everywhere. It has no clearly defined banks and no clearly defined direction. God wants us to be rivers not swamps.

In Acts 2 we often quote verses 38 and 39 but leave off 40. After the instruction to repent, and be baptized, Peter ended his message with this sentence. "Save yourselves from this untoward generation."

We live in a day of "untoward" things. Strong's Dictionary tells me this particular word means "warped" or "winding." If you know where you are going, and keep that goal in sight, then the possibilities of taking a winding road to get there are diminished. That your sense of accomplishment would be warped into pursuing lesser goals significantly diminishes. You must learn to say "no" to the trivial and "yes" to the important. You must say "no" to the temporal and a resounding "yes" to the eternal. The Apostle Paul said in Philippians 3:13-14:

> *Brethren, I count myself to have apprehended: but this one thing I do forgetting those things which are before, I press toward the mark for the prize of the high calling of God in Christ Jesus.*

Set your goal. Define your role. Pay the toll. You need to know where you want to go.

Loyalty is productive.

G. K. Chesterton observed, "We are all in the same boat on a stormy sea. We owe each other a terrible loyalty." My reputation should be the safest in your hands. Loyalty to our Lord involves being as faithful to your lifestyle and message outside of church, privately, as you are in church, publicly before a crowd. It involves language and attitudes toward God and others that are always consistent. Can you be counted on to be there - good times or bad? The term is "loyal to a fault" – Are you?

One writer said, "The most important ability is responsibility." Nothing happens until someone steps forward and says, "You can count on me" and means it. The best helping hand you will ever find is at the end of your own arm. Always faithfully reach out to others. "Here I am. Send me." should be our prayer – not, "There he is, send him."

One writer said, ""Your truest friends are the ones who will stand by you in your darkest moments--because they're willing to brave the shadows with you--and in your greatest moments--because they're not afraid to let you shine." Loyalty, at its finest, is just that . . . it is dark moments and braving shadows, and it is standing in the shadow to allow another to shine, without fear, celebrating with them their grandest accomplishments.

Martin Luther observed, ""Where the battle rages, there the loyalty of the soldier is proved." You will never know how loyal you are until you are given an opportunity to be disloyal. Loyalty will always cost you something and you never know just how loyal you are until you are required to pay for it.

We find in the story of Joseph the power of loyalty and its reward. Joseph had to buy into the dreams of three other fellas before his own came true. I've often wondered whether each of those junctures were turning points for Joseph. What if, in the moment when first the butler and then the baker shared their prison dreams with him, what if Joseph had chosen to shrug his shoulders and remain silent? Or what if he liked the butler better than the baker, and he had interpreted one dream and not the other? Would he have ever been given the opportunity to interpret the dream of Pharoah? And even then, what if he had gone silent before Pharoah and said, "You threw me in prison! Why should I do one thing for you?!" Joseph was loyal to his gifting and calling – He was loyal to his fellow-workers who became fellow-prisoners – He was loyal to his Pharoah.

The story in Genesis 40 tells us that Joseph was actually given charge over the butler and the baker. According to verse 4, "…and he served them." Something happens when you are loyal to those you serve. The King James text goes on to tell us that on that particular morning, Joseph noticed that both the butler and the baker were sad and asked, "Wherefore look ye so sadly to day?" They responded by sharing their respective dreams, which Joseph, in turn interpreted. He didn't skewer the answers, or manipulate the terms. He simply shared the interpretation God gave him for their dreams. It was after that Pharoah called for him to interpret one of his dreams . . .and the acts of loyalty that were a part of Joseph's life brought him promotion in that kingdom – and ultimately allowed him to be used to save a nation.

> *To be productive, I must be responsible.*

One author said, "Our background and circumstances may have influenced who we are but we are responsible for who we will become." I have often taught that who we are is God's gift to us. Who we become is our gift to God. God can do more through one man who is 100% dedicated than through 100 men who are 90% dedicated. Responsibility and dedication to the cause of the Gospel brings about productivity in the things of the Kingdom.

I have heard people blame their background, their birth, their environment for what they have become. Those things may determine what you are, but what you become is your responsibility – and with no excuses. For every person who has remained trapped in the chains of their background and upbringing, what happened to them or what didn't, there is another person who overcame the very same obstacles to become resounding successes in various areas of life. The abused woman has become a remarkable gifted counselor to abused children. The man raised in abject poverty paid his way through college and has become a respected financial advisor. The child raised on junk food has become a healthy-cooking chef.

One of the strongest spiritual examples of this we find in the story of Paul. Saul of Tarsus, who held the robes of the men who stoned Stephen and killed Christians, became Paul, the one who wrote most of the New Testament. He could have allowed who he was – the persecutor and killer of believers – to make him guilty and non-productive. Instead, he became responsible – responsible for sharing his story, sharing what Jesus Christ did for him with saints and sinners alike. He wrote, "Christ Jesus came into the world to save sinners; of whom I am chief." The chiefest of sinners became one of the greatest proclaimers of the Gospel.

It is the reality of virtually every church of every size: There is no shortage of opportunities to be productive. In being truly productive, you must take responsibility. In fact, being responsible will make you productive. If you are responsible for turning on the lights at your local church on Sundays, and you take your responsibility seriously, you will get up early and be at the church with all the switches in the "on" position when the first person walks in. How is that productive? You are doing your part to make everyone's Sunday church experience positive. That's responsibility. That's productivity.

David, that man after God's own heart, was seen first following the "ewes great with young." He was proving himself responsible in smaller duties. He ultimately became productive in Kingdom things. Psalms 78:70-72 tells us the story:

> *He chose David also his servant,*
> *and took him from the sheepfolds:*
> *From following the ewes great*
> *with young he brought him to feed*
> *Jacob his people, and Israel his*
> *inheritance. So he fed them*
> *according to the integrity of his*
> *heart; and guided them by the*
> *skillfulness of his hands.*

David exampled productivity and responsibility in his care of the sheep – and in his care of God's children when he became their king.

> *Not all the old is out of date nor is all the new acceptable.*

Jesus said, "The Kingdom of heaven is like unto a man that is a householder which bringeth forth out of his treasure things new and old" (Matthew 13:52). You have to know – to learn to discern - what is a treasure and what is just a utilitarian device. Everything in the house is not a treasure. If it matters little, make little of the matter.

Having this knowledge you go into the house and know the treasure that is to be brought forth. The original for "brought forth" means "scattered abroad lavishly." We don't hoard it - we scatter it - we share it.

There's an old adage about friendship that says, "Make new friends but keep the old. One is silver, the other gold." Be careful in choosing your friends – and in losing your friends. Friendship takes work and sometimes it takes hard work. However, it is worth the effort to maintain the friendship of one who will step into your world, when everything has gone wrong, and everyone else has walked away. I'm not saying not to develop new friendships. They are valuable and can bring new dimensions into our lives. Just be careful that you do not automatically discount the old and treasure the new. The new friends are not proven friends until you've been through some things together and they've been faithful and loyal and true.

In church life, people will resist change and will reject sudden change. In the Louisiana District, with its deep southern culture, I have often advised a new pastor that if he wants to move the piano he would be wise to move it one inch at a time. Perhaps the disparity between old and new is rarely more obvious than in the selection of songs for any given service. There was, in the church I attended as a boy, the Broadman Hymnal that contained such songs as "A Mighty Fortress is Our God" and "Come Thou Fount of Every Blessing." Upon joining the Pentecostal church, the songs there were less often the hymns of my childhood and were the more exultant songs of praise to a God who "brought me out the deep miry clay." Through the years I have watched and heard as music has gone through various phases of change. Now we have the modern worship choruses. While they are not my favorite, I am learning their value. Just because they're new does not give them value – nor does it devalue them in any way. The older hymns cannot be valued only because they are old, but must be respected for their content of Biblical doctrine and divine truth. The newer songs of worship cannot be disrespected, even with their repeated lyrics and replicated melody lines, because they are new. "Our God IS awesome!" I must learn to find the value in both.

There is a difference between cultural accommodation and eternal truth. We cannot put a gate where God has placed a fence – nor vice versa. Opinions are bountiful; principles are few. We must respect what God has set in place for us. We respect and honor His Word. Guard rails are usually set a few yards away from the precipice. Ignore them, though, and you are going down. That's another lesson I've learned in life.

> *Cherish the treasures of the past.*

What are they? The old things, no doubt - the message we have preached - is a rich treasure. Don't cheapen it or put it on sale. This is no day to put our message of the Book of Acts in the garage sale or flea market. In addition, we must recognize the history of any movement includes a constant openness to new and fresh stirrings of the Spirit. Our treasure finds its roots in the past. The root may be old, however, the fruit must be new and relevant. If there are no roots, there will be no fruit.

Proverbs 4:7 tells us, "Wisdom is the principal thing; therefore get wisdom: and with all thy getting get understanding." To be without wisdom is to lack understanding. It is the recipe for shipwreck.

Have you ever heard the story of "Four Feet and Eight and A Half Inches"? That is the standard space between train rails. Why? Because the people who built the first railroads in America were actually men from England who had come to the new country and that's how the English built trail tracks.

Why did the English use that gauge? Because before there were trains there were trams – and the trams used the same equipment they used to build wagons to build trams and thus 4'8" was the gauge of choice. Why were wagons spaced at that particular measure? Because in old England, the roads retained the ruts from old Roman chariots. These deep ruts would break a wagon wheel that did not fit in the rut. So, our United States standard railroad gauge, set by the original specifications for an Imperial Roman war chariot, is what, in fact, dictated that the dimensions of the standard booster rockets used for space travel. For you see, those SBRs have to be transported by train from Utah to the launch site via train and have to fit through tunnels that are gauged to 4-feet and 8-1/2 inches of space. Sometimes the things of the past have a keen relevance today.

There is value in old landmarks. Proverbs 22:28 cautions and instructs: "Remove not the ancient landmark, which thy fathers have set." Paul in writing to the Romans referred to serving: "…in newness of spirit, and not in the oldness of the letter." There is a keen balance in treasuring the landmarks of old, yet not walking in the oldness of the letter of the law. The key is the direction of the Holy Spirit. We walk in newness of life; we treasure the price that was paid for us to receive it.

> *There is no time or place in life where prayer can be eliminated.*

Carnality follows hard on the heels of prayerlessness. If you are too busy to pray, you are too busy. Jesus left the multitudes to go up into the mountains and pray. The pressure of the multitudes would probably beckon us to some different occupation. You will only be remembered in life by your passions. Have a passion for prayer!

In the early years of my Christian life I was taught and strived to pray one hour each day. For many years I maintained this discipline. However, as I grew in my walk with God, I can say that today – from the vantage point of nearly 80 years of age – there is rarely ever a time I pray a solid hour. More importantly, though, there is rarely an hour that goes by in which I do not pray.

Jesus exampled prayer. The Gospel accounts tell us of many times when He separated from His disciples and other followers and went to the mountain or some other solitary place to pray. Jesus said, "When you pray . . . " He did not say, "If . . . "

Jesus gave us, in Matthew 26:41, a reason to pray: "Watch and pray, that ye enter not into temptation: the spirit indeed is willing, but the flesh is weak."

He told us what and who to pray for:

...them which despitefully use you... (Matthew 5:44)

laborers for the harvest (Matthew 9:38)

...that your flight not be in winter... (Mark 13:18)

...that ye may be accounted worthy to escape all these things that shall come to pass, and to stand before the Son of man (Luke 21:36)

that ye enter not into temptation (Luke 22:40)

When asked "teach us to pray", He gave them – and us – a pattern for prayer (Luke 11:2-4):

> *And he said unto them, When ye pray, say, Our Father which art in heaven, Hallowed be thy name. Thy kingdom come. Thy will be done, as in heaven, so in earth. Give us day by day our daily bread. And forgive us our sins; for we also forgive every one that is indebted to us. And lead us not into temptation; but deliver us from evil.*

In Luke 18:1, Jesus teaches when to pray, "Men ought always to pray; and not to faint..."

And ultimately, He promised a response to our prayers: "And all things, whatsoever ye shall ask in **pray**er, believing, ye shall receive" (Matthew 21:22).

Prayer was the first administrative decision of the church after Pentecost – to set aside specific time for prayer and the Word.

We cannot allow the tyranny of the urgent to rob us of the time we must spend in prayer. We cannot allow our prayer to consist of fretting about circumstances. We must rather make sure our focus is on fellowship with the Father.

Jacob prayed and asked for a blessing. What he got was a life-changing wrestling match. To bring change, God had to put a death in him – touched his hip. Something dies within us every time we confront His glory. It's a handle for the holy. Nothing is fit to be offered until it is dead.

> *Be secure in yourself.*

I am not in competition with anyone. The only one I want to be better than is to be better than myself. I want to always recognize the different giftings that God gives. It has been observed that the secure are into towels; the insecure are into titles. The secure are people-conscious; the insecure are position-conscious.

The secure want to add value to others; the insecure want to receive value from others.

Don't waste time wishing you were someone else. Be the best you He called you to be. Know who you are. Know who He is. Know who He is in you and who you are in Him. The gifts you have been given by Him are yours to develop. Discover what they are. Work hard to hone your skills, to make each gift more effective and more valuable than it already is. Then, as the wise man of Proverbs reminds us: "⁶A man's gift maketh room for him, and bringeth him before great men" (Proverbs 18:16).

Knowing who you are and what your gifts are will make you comfortable in your own skin. It will strengthen confidence and dispel insecurity. There are few things as dangerous as an insecure preacher. His insecurity will drive him to say and do things a confident person would not do. More often than not, insecurity drapes itself in arrogance and over-confidence. These components can cause failure in all the relationships in your life.

Writer Robert Heinlein once wrote, "A competent and self-confident person is incapable of jealousy in anything. Jealousy is invariably a symptom of insecurity." Insecurity will give place to jealousy on many different levels. As we examine our own hearts, we can see that the place where we are least confident will be the most likely place for jealousy and envy to build their home on our insecurities.

Steven Furtick observed, ""The reason we struggle with insecurity is because we compare our behind-the-scenes with everyone else's highlight reel." We can be reassured by the words – a simple statement of truth – from the Psalmist: "He knoweth our frame." God created us, each and every one. We are His children, made in His image and likeness. We are not who the world says we are. We are not the labels others may have tried to place on us. We are His – and we are who He says we are. We are not defined by what happened to us or what people say about us. We are defined by the God who created, loved us, died for us, and is coming back for us.

The old song proclaims it, "Oh yes, oh yes, I'm a child of the King – and His royal blood now flows through my veins. And I who was wretched and poor now can sing, Praise God! Praise God! I'm a child of the King."

> *Respect is earned, not* demanded.

An election may give you the title of "Pastor" but only a servant's heart will give you that position in the lives of the people. If you have to constantly say, "I am the Pastor now you do what I demand of you..." you are already on the road to being on the losing side. You may direct their bodies but you will never lead their hearts. When the heart is separated from the body, death soon follows. There is nothing worse than the death of a relationship.

Yesterday's peacock is tomorrow's feather duster. Don't think more highly of yourself than others can think of you. Courtesy can be demanded. Courtesy is deserved. Respect, on the other hand, must be earned. Perhaps the first step toward earning respect is having it. Confucius said, "Respect yourself and others will respect you." The word and concept of balance appears again here. We must all learn to balance self-respect and true humility. Self-respect out of proportion takes on the qualities of arrogance which therby reduces self-respect to zero. It was Mahatma Ghandi who observed, "I cannot conceive of a greater loss than the loss of one's self-respect."

Jesus was not into titles; He was more into towels.

He gave clear instruction about the titles of His day in Matthew 23:8-11:

> *But be not ye called Rabbi: for one is your Master, even Christ; and all ye are brethren.*

And call no man your father upon the earth: for one is your Father, which is in heaven. Neither be ye called masters: for one is your Master, even Christ. But he that is greatest among you shall be your servant.

Are you a man or woman called to the role of Pastor? Are you called to be a Christian, whatever your role? Regardless of your answer, the call of God to individuals today is a call to servanthood not prominence. It is a call to take up a towel and kneel. It is the gift of redemption, not the weight of perfection.

> *Truth never changes.*

Regardless of how people change, cultures change, theories change - Truth remains. Not only does it remain but it is narrow. 2x2 still equals 4. Water still freezes at 32-degrees and boils at 212. There's no need to argue for any other way. It's narrow but it's true. So it is with God's infallible Word. What is written, is written. What is, is. Nothing can change truth. Time nor circumstance, light or darkness, love or hate, nothing makes truth any more or any less than what it is – truth.

I have learned, too, that with reference to the Word, when some people say they are standing for the truth, they are only standing for their interpretation of the truth.

It is often attributed to Augustine, but some researchers have determined it comes from an obscure and perhaps undistinguished German Lutheran theologian named Rupertus Meldenius. This simple quote from the 17th century is remarkably pertinent today: "In essentials, unity – in non-essentials, liberty – with charity above all." Truth is truth – irrefutable and unchanging. However, there are some "non-essentials" that, in fact, are not necessarily infallible truth, but instead are the things whereby we can extend liberty to each other without creating division. His truth is marching on.

> *I've never been sorry for things I didn't say.*

Too often the effectiveness of an idea or of words is dependent upon the temper of the times into which they are introduced. You can be right in an idea and wrong in its administration

It is wise to determine who built the fire – and what they used to build it – before you gather around it and join the conversation. Though Peter had verbalized a complete and total commitment to Jesus Christ – proclaimed Him to be the Son of the living God and followed Him to Gethsemane, Peter found himself gathered around an unfamiliar fire, with a group of unfamiliar "friends" denying Christ.

Beware of being used. Don't speak without determining whether or not the person spoken to – or those within hearing distance – are "quoters" or worse, "misquoters." Identify those who want to stand too close to you for the sole purpose of exploiting the "friendship" that, in fact, is not friendship at all.

Remember this: Gossip is halitosis of the brain. A gossip knows how to turn an earful into a mouthful. Avoid the person who gossips regardless of the disguise they wear, or place on their words and tales. How often has a twisted or even pure untruth been shared under the disguise of a prayer request: "Pray for Sue. You know her child is on drugs and is in jail for robbing the bank. I hear it's caused problems in her marriage."

Someone observed, "Throughout human history, our greatest leaders and thinkers have used the power of words to transform our emotions, to enlist us in their causes, and to shape the course of destiny. Words not only create emotions, they create actions. And from our actions flow the results of our lives." The Bible speaks of the beauty of a "word fitly spoken." Choose your words carefully. Speak them only after careful thought, knowing the power and effect words can have not only on the person who speaks them but also on those who hear them and take them to heart. One word – fitly spoken – can change someone's life.

The Psalmist prayed, "Let the words of my mouth, and the meditation of my heart, be acceptable in thy sight, O Lord, my strength, and my redeemer" (Psalm 19:14). So must we, today, be prayerful and careful about not only what we do, but about what we say, how we say it, and to whom we say it.

> *Submission is a mandate of God.*

Submission. No one escapes its blessings or its judgment. Abraham submitted to Mt. Moriah. Moses submitted, after leading the children of Israel for forty years, to death on Nebo without ever entering the promised land. Because He submitted to the cross, Jesus is the Savior of the world. Abraham is the father of the faithful. Moses is known as the Giver of the Law.

I worry about preachers who preach submission, while personally being truly accountable to no one. They say they are submitted to this person or that. In fact, they are submitted perhaps to the limit of discussion but never to the degree that brings action. They will wander the halls at conferences, meander in and out at Camp Meetings, sit in critical judgment on a message whose flavor they don't like, and even occasionally give their tongue to vicious criticism and gossip. Cross them, call them into accountability, and see what happens. Thank God, not all, but there are some who are absolutely not accountable to anyone under any circumstances. Beware the unsubmitted ones among us.

If I had to sum up the Bible in just one word it would be this one: Submission.

Brother Tenney, how can I know if I am submitted? You know you are submitted to God, when He asks you to do something you don't want to do and you do it. You know you are submitted to your Pastor when He asks you not to do something you want to do, and you don't do it.

No one strikes a match and lights a burning bush; God is the only igniter of one of those. Fire does not fall on empty altars.

On some tomorrow, when we stand before God, He is simply going to ask, "What did you do with the ones solitary life you were given?" Did you submit it back to God for use in His Kingdom in His way? Or did you, like Frank Sinatra, strive to do it your way?

Jesus demonstrated ultimate submission in the Garden of Gethsemane when He prayed and asked that the cup be removed from Him, then said, "…nevertheless not my will, but thine, be done…" (Luke 22:42).

Submission is scriptural. From submission to one another – wives to husbands – to the church to Christ, we must live submitted lives. We submit first and foremost to God. James had a keen insight into the principle of submission when he wrote: "But he giveth more grace. Wherefore he saith, God resisteth the proud, but giveth grace unto the humble. Submit yourselves therefore to God. Resist the devil, and he will flee from you. Draw nigh to God, and he will draw nigh to you" (James 4:6-7). True Biblical submission to God will bring grace and humility to the submitted one. True submission drives the enemy away and brings God near.

In Ephesians and in Hebrews we read the mandate of submission one to another:

> *Giving thanks for all things unto God and the father in the name of our Lord Jesus Christ; …submitting yourselves one to another in the fear of God…* (Ephesians 5:20-21).

> *Obey them that have the rule over you, and submit yourselves: for they watch for your souls,*

as they that must give account, that they may do it with joy, and not with grief…(Hebrews 13:17).

Paul spoke of wives being in submission to their husbands in Ephesians 5. Let me interject here that this is not a one-sided commandment. There are specific instructions as well to husbands with phrases like "love your wives, even as Christ loved the church, and gave Himself for it" (verse 25) and "So ought men to love their wives as their own bodies…" (verse 28) and again in verse 33, "…let everyone of you in particular so love his wife as himself."

Submission is an outflow of love. As Christ loved the church, we, in turn return our love to Him by our submission to His will and plan for our lives, and to His commandments about living our lives. John records Jesus saying to the disciples in one of His final discourses before the cross, "If ye love me, keep my commandments" (John 14:15). Submission to Him, love for Him, makes us commandment keepers. Submission is a mandate of God.

> *My wife is my best friend; my family is my dearest earthly treasure.*

As a pastor and a preacher, you have two roles with your children and your spouse. To your wife, you are pastor and spouse. To you children, you are their pastor and their father. The roles are similar in many ways, but greatly diverse in others. Work hardest on the role that will last the longest. Be sure when your wife needs the shoulder and sheltering arms of her husband, that you don't step into the role of "pastor" and expect her to respond to prayer and scripture.

The same goes for your children. Sometimes your children need you to be their pastor – to show them and explain to them the things of God and the Kingdom. It is incumbent upon you – as their pastor and as their father – to give them this spiritual guidance. On the other hand, sometimes the best thing you can do for your son is take off your tie and shoot some hoops. They need you to be their Dad. Never let any of them question which role comes first in your priorities. Be the head of your family. Be present as father. Be present as spouse. And, when the pastor is needed, be that as well. Just make sure when they need their Dad that the Pastor isn't who shows up.

It has been said that the best gift a man can give his children is to love their mother. Take the time to make sure not only that your wife knows that you love her – but that your children also see that she is important to you. Take the time for flowers and special gifts. Take her to dinner and don't talk church. Write her a letter or bring her a card. Call her for no other reason but to check on her and tell her you love her.

Sometimes you can give her an immeasurable gift by making the effort to share your thoughts with her. Men are headliners; women want details. Sometimes the greatest gift you can give her is simply to listen. Don't try to fix anything. Don't tell her what to do unless she finishes talking . . . takes a deep breath and asks, "So, what should I do?" Sometimes women just need a sounding board and you can be that for your wife and she will love you all the more for it!

As mentioned earlier, it is interesting that in Paul's writings he instructed wives to submit to their husbands, but the directives for husbands were about loving their wives. Love is imperative. You will still be a husband even when the day comes when you are no longer pastor. You will be father not only when the day comes when you are no longer pastor, but also when, perhaps, you are no longer husband.

Work hardest on the roles and relationships that last the longest. Someone is going to be at your bedside when you pass from this life to the next. When that day comes, you will not want it to be a random nurse or hired caregiver. You will want it to be your spouse and your children who hear your last words.

Lessons We've Learned

As I close our time together, I have a few more notes for your road of life. I hope sharing what I've learned will help you today, and in the days to come.

- ❖ I've learned failure is the opportunity to begin again more intelligently.

- ❖ Don't bother to give God instructions, just report for duty.

- ❖ Life is like an onion. You peel off one layer at a time and sometimes you weep.

- ❖ Ninety percent of the friction of daily life is caused by the wrong tone of voice.

- ❖ Nothing will ever be attempted if all possible objections must be overcome first.

- ❖ If you sow roses, you won't reap thorns.

- ❖ Before a man can wake up and find himself famous, he has to wake up and find himself.

- ❖ Bad temper merely shows lack of control and places you temporarily in the ranks of lunatics and fools.

- ❖ I shall allow no man to belittle my soul by making me hate him.

- ❖ He who cannot forgive others breaks the bridge

over which he himself must pass, for every man has the need to be forgiven.

❖ There are two ways of being rich. One is to have all you want; the other is to be satisfied with what you have

❖ Joy is the most infallible sign of the presence of God.

❖ Follow peace with all men.

And, last but not least . . .

❖ *...thou shalt love the Lord thy God with all of your heart, soul, mind, and strength – and ...your neighbor as yourself.*

There you have it. These are just a few lessons I've learned while traveling and meandering down this stream called life, in the boat called Pentecost on my way to the city called the New Jerusalem. My prayer is that I will continue to learn and some day hear Him say, "Well done...."

ABOUT THE TENNEYS

In 2005, after over sixty-five years of ministry, and well over fifty years of administrative work within the UPCI, T. F. Tenney became Bishop Emeritus of the Louisiana District and retired from full-time administrative work. He began his ministry at age 16 and married his sweetheart, in December of 1952, at the age of 19. They began their first pastorate in 1953. His ministry resume includes pastoring, serving as International Youth President, Executive Director of Foreign Missions, District Superintendent of Louisiana – along with serving on various Boards associated with that position including the General Board of the UPCI, Tupelo Children's Mansion Board of Directors, Lighthouse Ranch for Boys Board of Directors, and others. He was a radio speaker, both on a nationally broadcast radio program and a local daily program and was a respected writer and regular contributor to various religious periodicals. He authored thirteen books. A great joy to him was when he opened the United States Senate with prayer on his 80th birthday. He preached in over 115 nations of the world and was known for his wisdom, wit, big heart and big vision. He, and Thetus together, either started or brought to the forefront, Youth Camps, Sheaves for Christ, Youth Congress, Bible Quizzing, Partners in Missions, missionary and ministry retreats, Men and Women's

Conferences, and Youth Conferences within the UPCI. T. F. Tenney went to his eternal reward and rest on June 1, 2018, leaving his loved ones with the words "I'm in the presence of God."

Thetus Tenney has been involved in active Christian ministry for over seven decades. She began her ministry teaching children at the age of 15. After her marriage at age 18, Thetus worked tirelessly alongside her husband for 65 years. She is the author of several books, many of which have been translated into multiple languages, as well as the co-author, along with her son, of *How to Chase God While Chasing Kids*. Thetus founded the World Network of Prayer and served as the International Coordinator for many years. She has been involved in numerous righteous causes for our nation, hosted many conferences for women, and been involved in causes for youth and children. Thetus served on the Louisiana State Board of Education. She is currently conducting a "Play and Pray" ministry for preteen girls.

Thetus Tenney makes her home in Alexandria, Louisiana where she currently serves on staff at *The Pentecostals of Alexandria* and continues to maintain a speaking schedule. The Tenneys have two children, both involved, with their spouses, in full-time ministry. Thetus celebrates being "Mimi" to five wonderful grandchildren, a granddaughter-in-law, a grandson-in-law, and nine great grandchildren.

Made in the USA
Middletown, DE
13 March 2023